Cram101 Textbook Outlines to accompany:

Unfinished Nation : Concise History of the American People, Volume 1 : To 1877

Alan Brinkley, 5th Edition

A Cram101 Inc. publication (c) 2010.

PRACTICE EXAMS.

Get all of the self-teaching practice exams for each chapter of this textbook at **www.Cram101.com** and ace the tests. Here is an example:

Chapter 1

Unfinished Nation : Concise History of the American People, Volume 1 : To 1877
Alan Brinkley, 5th Edition,
All Material Written and Prepared by Cram101

I WANT A BETTER GRADE.   Items 1 - 50 of 100.

1 The _____ was a network of clandestine routes by which African slaves in the 19th century United States attempted to escape to free states, or as far north as Canada, with the aid of abolitionists. The _____ has captured public imagination as a symbol of freedom, and it figures prominently in Black American history.

○ Underground railroad   ○ U Go offensive

○ U S WEST, Inc.   ○ U Thong Style

2 _____ was the capital of the Aztec empire, built on an island in Lake Texcoco in what is now the Federal District in central Mexico. At its height, _____ was one of the largest cities in the world, with over 200,000 inhabitants. The city was destroyed in 1521 by Spanish conquistadors.

○ Tenochtitlan   ○ T and O map

○ T for Tibet   ○ T. A. Gillespie Company Shell Loading Plant explosion

3 _____ is the site of an ancient indigenous city near Collinsville, Illinois. In the American Bottom floodplain, it is across the Mississippi River from St. Louis, Missouri. The 2,200-acre (8.9 km^2) site included 120 man-made earthen mounds over an area of six square miles, although only 80 survive.

○ Cahokia   ○ C. Donald Shane telescope

○ C. R. Boxer   ○ C. Vijayaraghavachariar

4 The _____ (Afrikaans: Kaap die Goeie Hoop, Dutch: Â·), Portuguese: Cabo da Boa Esperança) is a rocky headland on the Atlantic coast of South Africa. There is a very common misconception that the _____ is the

You get a 50% discount for the online exams. Go to **Cram101.com**, click Sign Up at the top of the screen, and enter DK73DW8855 in the promo code box on the registration screen. Access to Cram101.com is $4.95 per month, cancel at any time.

With Cram101.com online, you also have access to extensive reference material.

You will nail those essays and papers. Here is an example from a Cram101 Biology text:

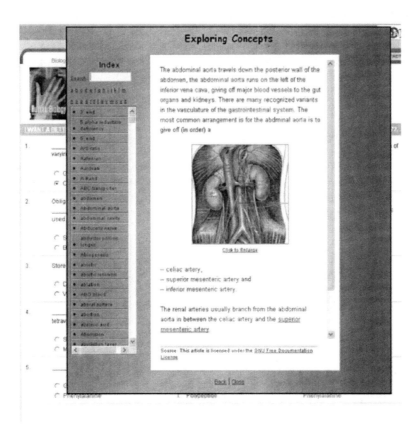

Visit **www.Cram101.com**, click Sign Up at the top of the screen, and enter DK73DW8855 in the promo code box on the registration screen. Access to www.Cram101.com is normally $9.95 per month, but because you have purchased this book, your access fee is only $4.95 per month, cancel at any time. Sign up and stop highlighting textbooks forever.

Learning System

Cram101 Textbook Outlines is a learning system. The notes in this book are the highlights of your textbook, you will never have to highlight a book again.

How to use this book. Take this book to class, it is your notebook for the lecture. The notes and highlights on the left hand side of the pages follow the outline and order of the textbook. All you have to do is follow along while your instructor presents the lecture. Circle the items emphasized in class and add other important information on the right side. With Cram101 Textbook Outlines you'll spend less time writing and more time listening. Learning becomes more efficient.

Cram101.com Online

Increase your studying efficiency by using Cram101.com's practice tests and online reference material. It is the perfect complement to Cram101 Textbook Outlines. Use self-teaching matching tests or simulate in-class testing with comprehensive multiple choice tests, or simply use Cram's true and false tests for quick review. Cram101.com even allows you to enter your in-class notes for an integrated studying format combining the textbook notes with your class notes.

Visit **www.Cram101.com**, click Sign Up at the top of the screen, and enter **DK73DW8855** in the promo code box on the registration screen. Access to www.Cram101.com is normally $9.95 per month, but because you have purchased this book, your access fee is only $4.95 per month. Sign up and stop highlighting textbooks forever.

Unfinished Nation : Concise History of the American People, Volume 1 : To 1877
Alan Brinkley, 5th

CONTENTS

Underground railroad	The Underground Railroad was a network of clandestine routes by which African slaves in the 19th century United States attempted to escape to free states, or as far north as Canada, with the aid of abolitionists. The Underground Railroad has captured public imagination as a symbol of freedom, and it figures prominently in Black American history.
Tenochtitlan	Tenochtitlan was the capital of the Aztec empire, built on an island in Lake Texcoco in what is now the Federal District in central Mexico. At its height, Tenochtitlan was one of the largest cities in the world, with over 200,000 inhabitants. The city was destroyed in 1521 by Spanish conquistadors.
Cahokia	Cahokia is the site of an ancient indigenous city near Collinsville, Illinois. In the American Bottom floodplain, it is across the Mississippi River from St. Louis, Missouri. The 2,200-acre (8.9 km^2) site included 120 man-made earthen mounds over an area of six square miles, although only 80 survive.
Cape of Good Hope	The Cape of Good Hope (Afrikaans: Kaap die Goeie Hoop, Dutch: Â·), Portuguese: Cabo da Boa Esperança) is a rocky headland on the Atlantic coast of South Africa. There is a very common misconception that the Cape of Good Hope is the southern tip of Africa and the dividing point between the Atlantic and Indian Oceans, but in fact the southernmost point is Cape Agulhas, about 150 kilometres (90 mi) to the east-southeast. However, when following the coastline from the equator, the Cape of Good Hope marks the psychologically important point where one begins to travel more eastward than southward.
Vasco da Gama	Dom Vasco da Gama 1st Count of Vidigueira (Portuguese pronunciation: [Ëˆvaɐ̂ʃku dɉ Ëˆɉ¡ɉɒmɉɒ]) (Sines or Vidigueira, Alentejo, Portugal, ca. either 1460 or 1469 - December 24, 1524 in Kochi, India) was a Portuguese explorer, one of the most successful in the European Age of Discovery and the commander of the first ships to sail directly from Europe to India. For a short time in 1524 he was Governor of Portuguese India under the title of Viceroy.
Philippines	The Philippines, is an island country located in Southeast Asia with Manila as its capital city. The Philippines comprises 7,107 islands in the western Pacific Ocean, sharing maritime borders with Indonesia, Malaysia, Palau, the Republic of China, and Vietnam. The Philippines is the world"s 12th most populous country with a population of 90 million people.
Typhus	Typhus is any of several similar diseases caused by Rickettsiae The name comes from the Greek typhos, meaning smoky or hazy, describing the state of mind of those affected with typhus. The causative organism Rickettsia is an obligate parasite and cannot survive for long outside living cells. Typhus should not be confused with Typhoid Fever which is a completely different disease.
Thomas Paine	Thomas Paine was a pamphleteer, revolutionary, radical intellectual, and deist. He lived in America having emigrated to the American colonies just in time for him to take part in the American Revolution, mainly as the author of the powerful and widely read pamphlet Common Sense, which advocated independence from the Kingdom of Great Britain.

3

Predestination	*Predestination* (also linked with foreknowledge) is a religious concept, which involves the relationship between God and His creation. The religious character of *Predestination* distinguishes it from other ideas about determinism and free will. Those who believe in *Predestination*, such as John Calvin, believe that before the creation God determined the fate of the universe throughout all of time and space.
Protestantism	*Protestantism* is a Christian protest movement originating in the early 16th century in Germany opposing Roman Catholicism. *Protestantism* encompasses the forms of Christian faith and practice that originated with the doctrines of the Reformation.
Reformation	The Reformation was a movement in the 16th century to reform the Catholic Church in Western Europe. Many western Christians were troubled by what they saw as false doctrines and malpractices within the Church, particularly involving the teaching and sale of indulgences. Another major contention was the tremendous corruption within the Church"s hierarchy, all the way up to the Bishop of Rome, who appointed individuals to various positions within the Church on the basis of financial contributions.
Separatism	Separatism is a term usually applied to describe the attitudes or motivations of those seeking independence or "separation" of their land or region from the country that governs them. To a lesser extent, separatism may also refer to social isolation or involvement in cliques.
Dutch West India Company	Dutch West India Company was a chartered company of Dutch merchants. Among its founding fathers was Willem Usselincx . On June 3, 1621, it was granted a charter for a trade monopoly in the West Indies (meaning the Caribbean) by the Republic of the Seven United Netherlands and given jurisdiction over the African slave trade, Brazil, the Caribbean, and North America.
New Amsterdam	New Amsterdam was the 17th century Dutch colonial town that later became New York City.
New Netherland	New Netherland 1614–1674, was the territory on the eastern New Netherland coast of North America in the 17th century which stretched from latitude 38 to 45 degrees North as originally discovered by the Dutch East India Company with the yacht Half Moon under the command of Henry Hudson in 1609 and explored by Adriaen Block and Hendrick Christiaensz from 1611 through 1614.
Spanish Armada	The Spanish Armada was the Spanish fleet that sailed against England under the command of the Duke of Medina Sidonia in 1588, leading to the Drake-Norris Expedition of 1589, also known as the English Armada. King Philip II of Spain had been king consort of England until the death, in 1558, of his wife, Queen Mary I of England, and he took exception to the policies pursued by her successor, his sister-in-law Elizabeth I. The aim of his expedition was to invade and conquer England, thereby suppressing support for the United Provinces--that part of the Low Countries not under Spanish domination--and cutting off attacks by the English against Spanish possessions in the New World and against the Atlantic treasure fleets.

Saint Lawrence river	*Saint Lawrence river* is a large river flowing approximately from southwest to northeast in the middle latitudes of North America, connecting the Great Lakes with the Atlantic Ocean. It is the primary drainage of the Great Lakes Basin. It traverses the Canadian provinces of Quebec and Ontario and forms part of the international boundary between Ontario, Canada, and the U.S. state of New York.
Roanoke colony	The Roanoke Colony on Roanoke Island in Dare County in present-day North Carolina was an enterprise financed and organized by Sir Walter Raleigh in the late 16th century to establish a permanent English settlement in the Virginia Colony. Between 1585 and 1587, groups of colonists were left to make the attempt. The final group disappeared after a period of three years elapsed without supplies from England, leading to the continuing mystery known as "The Lost Colony."

Chapter 2. Transplantations and Borderlands

London Company	The London Company (also called the Charter of the Virginia Company of London) was an English joint stock company established by royal charter by James I of England on April 10, 1606 with the purpose of establishing colonial settlements in North America. It was not founded as a joint stock company, but became one under the 1609 charter. It was one of two such companies, along with the Plymouth Company, that was granted an identical charter as part of the Virginia Company.
Virginia Company	The Virginia Company refers collectively to a pair of English joint stock companies chartered by James I in 1606 with the purposes of establishing settlements on the coast of North America. The Virginia Company also helped establish trade and tobacco which led to great wealth for early colonies.
Virginia	The Commonwealth of Virginia is an American state on the Atlantic Coast of the Southern United States. The state was named Virginia after Queen Elizabeth I of England, who was known as the "Virgin Queen" because she never married. The state is also known as the "Old Dominion" and sometimes "Mother of Presidents", because it is the birthplace of eight U.S. presidents.
Pocahontas	Pocahontas was a Native American woman who married an Englishman, John Rolfe, and became a celebrity in London toward the end of her life. The records of the Jamestown settlers indicate that Pocahontas had a friendship of some kind with Captain John Smith, and may have saved him from death more than once.
Pilgrims	The Pilgrims were a group of English religious separatists who sailed from Europe to North America in the early 17th century, in search of a home where they could freely practice their Puritan style of religion and live according to their own laws.
Plymouth Company	The Plymouth Company was an English joint stock company founded in 1606 by James I of England with the purpose of establishing settlements on the coast of North America.
Separatism	Separatism is a term usually applied to describe the attitudes or motivations of those seeking independence or "separation" of their land or region from the country that governs them. To a lesser extent, separatism may also refer to social isolation or involvement in cliques.
Mayflower	The Mayflower was the famous ship that transported the English Separatists, better known as the Pilgrims, from Southampton, England, to Plymouth, Massachusetts , in 1620. The vessel left England on September 6 (Old Style)/September 16 (New Style), and after a gruelling 66-day journey marked by disease, which claimed two lives, the ship dropped anchor inside the hook tip of Cape Cod (Provincetown Harbor) on November 11/November 21. The Mayflower was originally destined for the mouth of the Hudson River, near present-day New York City, at the northern edge of England"s Virginia colony, which itself was established with the 1607 Jamestown Settlement.
Mayflower Compact	The Mayflower Compact was the first governing document of Plymouth Colony. It was written by the colonists, later together known to history as the Pilgrims, who crossed the Atlantic aboard the Mayflower. Almost half of the colonists were part of a separatist group seeking the freedom to practice Christianity according to their own determination and not the will of the English Church.

Massachusetts Bay Colony	The Massachusetts Bay Colony (sometimes called the Massachusetts Bay Company, for the institution that founded it) was an English settlement on the east coast of North America in the 17th century, in New England, centered around the present-day cities of Salem and Boston. The area is now in the Commonwealth of Massachusetts, one of the 50 United States of America. Plans for the first permanent European settlements on the east coast of North America began in 1606, when King James I of England formed two joint stock companies.
Thomas Hooker	Thomas Hooker, was a prominent Puritan religious and colonial leader remembered as one of the founders of the Colony of Connecticut. In 1636, Thomas Hooker led his congregation west to found the new English settlement at Hartford, Connecticut. One of the reasons he left Massachusetts was his failure to agree with John Winthrop about who should take part in civil government.
Religious toleration	*Religious toleration* is the condition of accepting or permitting others" religious beliefs and practices which disagree with one"s own. In a country with a state religion, toleration means that the government permits religious practices of other sects besides the state religion, and does not persecute believers in other faiths. It is a partial status, and might still be accompanied by forms of religious discrimination.
Oliver Cromwell	Oliver Cromwell (25 April 1599 Old Style– 3 September 1658 Old Style) was an English military and political leader best known for his involvement in making England into a republican Commonwealth and for his later role as Lord Protector of England, Scotland, and Ireland. He was one of the commanders of the New Model Army which defeated the royalists in the English Civil War.
Carolina	The Carolina s is a term used in the United States to refer collectively to the states of North and South Carolina The Carolina s were known as the Province of Carolina during America"s colonial period, from 1663-1710. Prior to that, the land was considered part of the Colony and Dominion of Virginia, from 1609-63.
Port Royal	Port Royal was the centre of shipping commerce in Jamaica in the 17th century. During this time, it gained a reputation as both the "richest and wickedest city in the world".
New Amsterdam	New Amsterdam was the 17th century Dutch colonial town that later became New York City.
New Netherland	New Netherland 1614–1674, was the territory on the eastern New Netherland coast of North America in the 17th century which stretched from latitude 38 to 45 degrees North as originally discovered by the Dutch East India Company with the yacht Half Moon under the command of Henry Hudson in 1609 and explored by Adriaen Block and Hendrick Christiaensz from 1611 through 1614.
Predestination	*Predestination* (also linked with foreknowledge) is a religious concept, which involves the relationship between God and His creation. The religious character of *Predestination* distinguishes it from other ideas about determinism and free will. Those who believe in *Predestination*, such as John Calvin, believe that before the creation God determined the fate of the universe throughout all of time and space.

Spanish colonization	The Spanish colonization of the Americas began with the arrival in the Western Hemisphere of Christopher Columbus in 1492. From early small settlements in the Caribbean, the Spanish gradually expanded their range over four centuries to include Central America, most of South America, Mexico, parts of what today is Southern United States and the Central United States, the Southwestern part of what today is British Columbia in Canada, and even reaching Alaska, eventually ending with a series of independence movements in the Nineteenth Century, including ultimately Cuba and Puerto Rico in 1898 as part of the Spanish-American War.
Louisiana	The State of Louisiana ; French: État de Louisiane, [lwizjan] ; Louisiana Creole: Léta de la Lwizyàn) is a state located in the southern region of the United States of America. Its capital is Baton Rouge and largest city is New Orleans. Louisiana is the only state divided into parishes, which are local governments equivalent to counties.
Francis Parkman	Francis Parkman (September 16, 1823 - November 8, 1893) was an American historian, best known as author of The Oregon Trail: Sketches of Prairie and Rocky-Mountain Life and his monumental seven volume France and England in North America. These works are still valued as history and especially as literature, although the biases of his work have met with criticism. He was also a leading horticulturist, briefly a Professor of Horticulture at Harvard University and the first leader of the Arnold Arboretum, and author of several books on the topic.
Navigation Acts	The English Navigation Acts were a series of laws which, beginning in 1651, restricted foreign shipping. Resentment against the Navigation Acts was a cause of the Anglo-Dutch Wars and the American Revolutionary War.
Dominion of New England	The Dominion of New England in America (1686-89) was a short-lived administrative union of English colonies in the New England region of North America. King James II of England decreed the creation of the Dominion as a measure to enforce the Navigation Acts and to coordinate the mutual defense of colonies against the French and hostile Native Americans. The Dominion initially comprised the Massachusetts Bay Colony, the Plymouth Colony, the Province of New Hampshire, the Province of Maine, and the Narraganset Country or King"s Province.

Middle passage	The Middle Passage refers to the forcible passage of African people from Africa to the New World, as part of the Atlantic slave trade. Ships departed Europe for African markets with commercial goods, which were in turn traded for kidnapped Africans who were transported across the Atlantic as slaves; the enslaved Africans were then sold or traded as commodities for raw materials, which would be transported back to Europe to complete the "triangular trade". The term Middle Passage refers to that middle leg of the transatlantic trade triangle in which millions of Africans were imprisoned, enslaved, and removed from their homelands.
Royal African Company	The Royal African Company was a slaving company set up by the Stuart family and London merchants once the former retook the English throne in the English Restoration of 1660. It was led by James, Duke of York, Charles II"s brother. Originally known as the Company of Royal Adventurers Trading to Africa, it was granted a monopoly over the English slave trade, by its charter issued in 1660.
Slave Codes	Slave codes were laws passed in colonial North America to regulate any state of subjection to a force, and were abolished after the U.S. Civil War. Slave codes authorized, indemnified or even required the use of violence and were long criticized by abolitionists for their brutality.
Edict of Nantes	The Edict of Nantes (sometimes spelled Edict of Nantz) was issued on April 13, 1598. by Henry IV of France to grant the Calvinist Protestants of France (also known as Huguenots) substantial rights in a nation still considered essentially Catholic. The main concern was civil unity, and the Edict separated civil from religious unity, treated some Protestants for the first time as more than mere schismatics and heretics, and opened a path for secularism and tolerance.
Pennsylvania Dutch	Pennsylvania Dutch are the descendants of German immigrants who came to Pennsylvania prior to 1800.
Stono Rebellion	The Stono Rebellion is one of the earliest known organized acts of rebellion against slavery in the Americas. On September 9, 1739 South Carolina slaves gathered at the Stono River to plan an armed march for freedom.
Thomas Paine	Thomas Paine was a pamphleteer, revolutionary, radical intellectual, and deist. He lived in America having emigrated to the American colonies just in time for him to take part in the American Revolution, mainly as the author of the powerful and widely read pamphlet Common Sense, which advocated independence from the Kingdom of Great Britain.
Printing press	The printing press is a mechanical printing device for making copies of identical text on multiple sheets of paper. It was invented in Germany by the goldsmith Johannes Gutenberg in 1440.
Stamp Act	A stamp act is a law enacted by a government that requires a tax to be paid on the transfer of certain documents. Those that pay the tax receive an official stamp on their documents. The tax raised, called stamp duty, was first devised in the Netherlands in 1624 after a public competition to find a new form of tax.

Royal Society of London

The Royal Society of London for the Improvement of Natural Knowledge, known simply as The Royal Society, was founded in 1660 and claims to be the oldest learned society still in existence.

Louisiana	The State of Louisiana ; French: État de Louisiane, [lwizjan] ; Louisiana Creole: Léta de la Lwizyàn) is a state located in the southern region of the United States of America. Its capital is Baton Rouge and largest city is New Orleans. Louisiana is the only state divided into parishes, which are local governments equivalent to counties.
Treaty of Utrecht	The Treaty of Utrecht that established the Peace of Utrecht, rather than a single document, comprized a series of individual peace treaties signed in the Dutch city of Utrecht in March and April 1713. Concluded between various European states, it helped end the War of the Spanish Succession.
Fort Duquesne	Fort Duquesne (originally called Fort Du Quesne) was a fort established by the French in 1754, at the junction of the Allegheny and Monongahela rivers in what is now downtown Pittsburgh in the state of Pennsylvania. It was destroyed and replaced by Fort Pitt in 1758; over two centuries later, the site formerly occupied by Fort Duquesne is now Point State Park. 19th century illustration of Fort Duquesne by Alfred Waud. French forts, 1753 and 1754 The point where the Allegheny and Monongahela rivers merged to form the Ohio River was long seen as important for controlling the Ohio Country, both for settlement and for trade.
Pontiac	Pontiac was an Ottawa leader who became famous for his role in Pontiac"s Rebellion,1763 - 1766, an American Indian struggle against the British military occupation of the Great Lakes region following the British victory in the French and Indian War.
Paxton Boys	The Paxton Boys were a group of backcountry Scots-Irish frontiersmen from the area around the central Pennsylvania village of Paxtang, near present day Harrisburg, Pennsylvania, who formed a vigilante group in response to the American Indian uprizing known as Pontiac"s Rebellion. The Paxton Boys felt that the government of colonial Pennsylvania, dominated by Quaker pacifists, was negligent in providing them with protection, and so decided
Stamp Act	A stamp act is a law enacted by a government that requires a tax to be paid on the transfer of certain documents. Those that pay the tax receive an official stamp on their documents. The tax raised, called stamp duty, was first devised in the Netherlands in 1624 after a public competition to find a new form of tax.
Thomas Hutchinson	Thomas Hutchinson, was the American colonial governor of Massachusetts from 1771 to 1774 and a prominent Loyalist in the years before the American Revolutionary War.
Sons of Liberty	The Sons of Liberty was a label adopted by Patriots in the British North American colonies before the American Revolution. Latter-day historians have called them terrorists, a word that was coined during the French Revolution and has gained new meanings in recent decades.

Stamp Act congress	The Stamp Act Congress was a meeting in New York City in October 1765 of delegates from the American Colonies that discussed and acted upon the recently passed Stamp Act. The meetings adopted a Declaration of Rights and Grievances and wrote letters or petitions to the King and both houses of Parliament. This Congress is viewed by some as the first American action in or as a precursor to the American Revolution.
Virginia Resolves	The Virginia Resolves were a series of resolutions passed by the Virginia General Assembly in response to the Stamp Act of 1765.
Boston Massacre	The Boston Massacre was an incident that led to the deaths of five civilians at the hands of British troops on March 5, 1770, the legal aftermath of which helped spark the rebellion in some of the British American colonies, which culminated in the American Revolution. A tense situation because of a heavy British military presence in Boston boiled over to incite brawls between soldiers and civilians and eventually led to troops discharging their muskets after being attacked by a rioting crowd. Three civilians were killed at the scene of the shooting, and two died after the incident.
Presidency	Presidency is a title held by many leaders of organizations, companies, trade unions, universities, and countries. Etymologically, it is one who presides, who sits in leadership Originally, the term referred to the presiding officer of a ceremony or meeting; but today it most commonly refers to an official with executive powers.
Samuel Adams	Samuel Adams was the chief Massachusetts leader of the Patriot cause leading to the American Revolution. Organizer of protests including the Boston Tea Party, he was most influential as a writer and theorist who articulated the principles of republicanism that shaped the American political culture.
Boston Tea Party	The Boston Tea Party was a direct action by colonists in Boston, a town in the British colony of Massachusetts, against the British government. On December 16, 1773, after officials in Boston refused to return three shiploads of taxed tea to Britain, a group of colonists boarded the ships and destroyed the tea by throwing it into Boston Harbor. The incident remains an iconic event of American history, and has often been referenced in other political protests.
Quebec Act	While it is clear that the Quebec Act did much to secure the allegiance of the Canadians to Britain, it had other unforeseen consequences. It was termed one of the Intolerable Acts by the American colonists. The Act was never enforced outside Canada. Its main importance was to anger the Americans. weaken the King"s supporters (Loyalists) and speed the confrontation that became the American Revolution.

Chapter 5. The American Revolution

Samuel Adams	Samuel Adams was the chief Massachusetts leader of the Patriot cause leading to the American Revolution. Organizer of protests including the Boston Tea Party, he was most influential as a writer and theorist who articulated the principles of republicanism that shaped the American political culture.
Thomas Paine	Thomas Paine was a pamphleteer, revolutionary, radical intellectual, and deist. He lived in America having emigrated to the American colonies just in time for him to take part in the American Revolution, mainly as the author of the powerful and widely read pamphlet Common Sense, which advocated independence from the Kingdom of Great Britain.
Carl Lotus Becker	Carl Lotus Becker (1873-1945) was an American historian. He was born in Waterloo, Black Hawk County, Iowa. He studied at the University of Wisconsin-Madison.
Thomas Sumter	Thomas Sumter was a hero of the American Revolution and went on to become a longtime member of the Congress of the United States. He acquired the nickname, "The Carolina Gamecock" during the American Revolution for his fierce fighting tactics, regardless of his size.
Popular sovereignty	Popular sovereignty is the doctrine that government is created by and subject to the will of the people, who are the source of all political power.
Ottoman empire	The Ottoman Empire or Ottoman State , also known by its contemporaries as the Turkish Empire or Turkey , was an empire that lasted from 1299 to November 1, 1922 (as an imperial monarchy) or July 24, 1923 (de jure, as a state.) It was succeeded by the Republic of Turkey, which was officially proclaimed on October 29, 1923. At the height of its power (16th-17th century), it spanned three continents, controlling much of Southeastern Europe, Western Asia and North Africa.
Northwest Ordinance	The Northwest Ordinance was an act of the Continental Congress of the United States passed on July 13, 1787 under the Articles of Confederation. The primary effect of the ordinance was the creation of the Northwest Territory as the first organized territory of the United States out of the region south of the Great Lakes north and west of the Ohio River, and east of the Mississippi River. On August 7, 1789, the U.S. Congress affirmed the Ordinance with slight modifications under the Constitution.
Treaty of Greenville	The Treaty of Greenville was signed at Fort Greenville, on August 3, 1795, between a coalition of Native Americans and the United States following the Native American loss at the Battle of Fallen Timbers. It put an end to the Northwest Indian War.
Daniel Shays	Daniel Shays (c.1741 - September 29, 1825) is mostly known for leading an army of farmers in Shays" Rebellion, which was a tax revolt against the state government of Massachusetts from 1786-1787, and a key event in the early history of the United States. The rebellion underscored the weakness of the Articles of Confederation and played a significant part in the formation of the United States Constitution. Little is known of his early life although he was most likely born in Hopkinton, Massachusetts in 1741.

Philadelphia Convention	The Philadelphia Convention took place from May 25 to September 17, 1787, to address problems in The United States of America following independence from Great Britain. Although it was purportedly intended only to revise the Articles of Confederation, the intention of many of the Convention"s proponents, chief among them James Madison and Alexander Hamilton, was from the outset to create a new government rather than "fix" the existing one.
New Jersey Plan	The New Jersey Plan was a proposal for the structure of the United States Government proposed by William Paterson on June 15, 1787. The plan was created in response to the Virginia Plan"s call for two houses of Congress, both elected with proportional representation.
Virginia Plan	A proposal by Virginia delegates during the Constitutional Convention of 1787, the Virginia Plan was notable for its role in setting the overall agenda for debate in the convention and, in particular, for setting forth the idea of population-weighted representation in the proposed National Legislature.
Separation of powers	Separation of powers, or "Trias Politica" a term coined by French political Enlightenment thinker Baron de Montesquieu, is a model for the governance of democratic states. Under this model the state is divided into branches, and each branch of the state has separate and independent powers and areas of responsibility.
Popular sovereignty	Popular sovereignty is the doctrine that government is created by and subject to the will of the people, who are the source of all political power.
Samuel Adams	Samuel Adams was the chief Massachusetts leader of the Patriot cause leading to the American Revolution. Organizer of protests including the Boston Tea Party, he was most influential as a writer and theorist who articulated the principles of republicanism that shaped the American political culture.
Bill of Rights	In the United States, the Bill of Rights is the name by which the first ten amendments to the United States Constitution are known. They were introduced by James Madison to the First United States Congress in 1789 as a series of articles, and came into effect on December 15, 1791, when they had been ratified by three-fourths of the States. Thomas Jefferson was a proponent of the Bill of Rights
Northwest Ordinance	The Northwest Ordinance was an act of the Continental Congress of the United States passed on July 13, 1787 under the Articles of Confederation. The primary effect of the ordinance was the creation of the Northwest Territory as the first organized territory of the United States out of the region south of the Great Lakes north and west of the Ohio River, and east of the Mississippi River. On August 7, 1789, the U.S. Congress affirmed the Ordinance with slight modifications under the Constitution.
Aaron Burr	Aaron Burr Jr. (February 6, 1756 - September 14, 1836) was an American politician, Revolutionary War participant, and adventurer. He served as the third Vice President of the United States (1801-1805), under Thomas Jefferson.

Predestination	*Predestination* (also linked with foreknowledge) is a religious concept, which involves the relationship between God and His creation. The religious character of *Predestination* distinguishes it from other ideas about determinism and free will. Those who believe in *Predestination*, such as John Calvin, believe that before the creation God determined the fate of the universe throughout all of time and space.
Second Great Awakening	The Second Great Awakening was the second great religious revival in United States history and consisted of renewed personal salvation experienced in revival meetings. Major leaders included Charles Grandison Finney, Lyman Beecher, Barton Stone, Peter Cartwright and James B. Finley.
Unitarianism	Unitarianism is the belief in the oneness of God opposed to the Christian doctrine of the Trinity. Unitarians believe in the moral authority, but not the deity, of Jesus.
Samuel Slater	Samuel Slater was an early American industrialist popularly known as the "Founder of the American Industrial Revolution" because he brought British textile technology to America. By the end of his life he owned thirteen spinning mills.
Robert Fulton	Robert Fulton was a U.S. engineer and inventor, who was widely credited with developing the first steam-powered ship marked as a commercial success. In 1800 he was commissioned by Napoleon Bonaparte to design Nautilus, which was the first practical submarine in history.
Interchangeable parts	Interchangeable parts are parts that are for practical purposes identical. They are made to specifications that ensure that they are so nearly identical that they will fit into any device of the same type. One such part can freely replace another, without any custom fitting (such as filing.)
Marbury v. Madison	Marbury v. Madison 5 U.S. (1 Cranch) 137 (1803) is a landmark case in United States law This case resulted from a petition to the Supreme Court by William Marbury, who had been appointed by President John Adams as Justice of the Peace in the District of Columbia but whose commission was not subsequently delivered.
Morocco	Morocco officially the Kingdom of Morocco is a country located in North Africa with a population of nearly 32 million and an area just under 447,000 square kilometres (173,000 sq mi.) Its capital is Rabat, and its largest city is Casablanca. Morocco has a coast on the Atlantic Ocean that reaches past the Strait of Gibraltar into the Mediterranean Sea.
Tripoli	Tripoli - also Ø·Ø±Ø§Ø¨Ù„Ø³ Ø§Ù„ØºØ±Ø¨ á¹arÄ€-bu-lus al-Gharb Libyan vernacular: á¹rÄ›blÉ™s Â·); derived from the word for "three cities" in Greek: Τρί̄πολις Tripoli s) is the largest and capital city of Libya.
United States Military Academy	The United States Military Academy, also known as West Point, is a United States Army post and service academy. West Point was first a military post under the command of Benedict Arnold. Established in 1802, it is the oldest military academy in the United States.

Burr Conspiracy	The Burr conspiracy was a suspected treasonous cabal of planters, politicians and army officers led by former U.S. Vice President Aaron Burr. According to the accusations against him, Burr"s goal was to create an independent nation in the center of North America and/or the Southwest and parts of Mexico. Burr"s explanation: To take possession of, and farm, 40,000 acres (160 km^2) in the Texas Territory leased to him by the Spanish.
Essex Junto	The Essex Junto was a group of lawyers and merchants from Essex County, Massachusetts. These Federalists supported Alexander Hamilton and the Massachusetts radicals. When Hamilton was offered a place in the plot to secede New England from the Union, he denied the offer.
Sacajawea	Sacajawea was a Shoshone woman who accompanied the Corps of Discovery with Meriwether Lewis and William Clark in their exploration of the Western United States, traveling thousands of miles from North Dakota to the Pacific Ocean between 1804 and 1806. She was nicknamed Janey by some members of the expedition.
Aaron Burr	Aaron Burr Jr. (February 6, 1756 - September 14, 1836) was an American politician, Revolutionary War participant, and adventurer. He served as the third Vice President of the United States (1801-1805), under Thomas Jefferson.
Non-Intercourse Act	In the last days of President Thomas Jefferson"s presidency, the United States Congress replaced the Embargo Act of 1807 with the almost unenforceable Non-Intercourse Act of March 1809. This Act lifted all embargoes on American shipping except for those bound for British or French ports.
Tecumseh	Tecumseh was a famous Shawnee leader. He spent much of his life attempting to rally disperate Native American tribes in a mutual defense of their lands, which eventually culminated in his death in the War of 1812.
New England	New England is a region of the United States located in the northeastern corner of the country, bounded by the Atlantic Ocean, Canada and New York State, and consisting of the modern states of Maine, New Hampshire, Vermont, Massachusetts, Rhode Island, and Connecticut. In one of the earliest English settlements in the New World, English Pilgrims fleeing religious persecution in Europe first settled in New England in 1620, in the colony of Plymouth. In the late 18th century, the New England colonies would be among the first North American British colonies to demonstrate ambitions of independence from the British Crown, although they would later oppose the War of 1812 between the United States and Britain.
Hartford Convention	The Hartford Convention was an event in 1814-1815 in the United States during the War of 1812 in which New England"s opposition to the war reached the point where secession from the United States was discussed. The end of the war with a return to the status quo ante bellum disgraced the Federalist Party, which disbanded in most places. Thomas Jefferson"s anti-foreign trade policies, particularly the Embargo Act of 1807 and James Madison"s Non-Intercourse Act of 1809, were very unpopular in the northeastern United States, especially among merchants and shippers.

Rush-Bagot Treaty

The *Rush-Bagot Treaty* was a treaty between the United States and the United Kingdom enacted in 1817 (signed April 28-29, 1817 in Washington, DC.) The treaty provided for the demilitarization of the Great Lakes and Lake Champlain, where many British naval armaments and forts still remained. The treaty laid the basis for a demilitarized boundary between the U.S. and British North America. This agreement was indicative of improving relations between the United States and Great Britain in the period following the War of 1812.

30

Protectionism	Protectionism is the economic policy of restraining trade between nations, through methods such as high tariffs on imported goods, restrictive quotas, a variety of restrictive government regulations designed to discourage imports, and anti-dumping laws in an attempt to protect domestic industries in a particular nation from foreign take-over or competition. This is closely aligned with anti-globalization, and contrasts with free trade, where no artificial barriers to entry are instituted.
National Road	The National Road or Cumberland Road was one of the first major improved highways in the United States, built by the Federal Government. Construction began in 1811 at Cumberland, Maryland on the Potomac River, and the road reached Wheeling, West Virginia on the Ohio River in 1818. Plans were made to continue through St. Louis, Missouri on the Mississippi River to Jefferson City, Missouri, but funding ran out and construction stopped at Vandalia, Illinois in 1839.
Santa Fe Trail	The Santa Fe Trail was an historic 19th century transportation route across southwestern North America connecting Missouri with Santa Fe, New Mexico. First used in 1821 by William Becknell, it served as a vital commercial and military highway until the introduction of the railroad to Santa Fe in 1880.
Rocky Mountain Fur Company	The Rocky Mountain Fur Company, sometimes called Ashley"s Hundred, was organized in St. Louis, Missouri in 1823 by General William H. Ashley and Major Andrew Henry.
Era of Good Feeling	The Era of Good Feeling s (1817-25) describes a period in United States political history in which partisan bitterness abated. The phrase was coined by Benjamin Russell, in the Boston newspaper, Columbian Centinel, on July 12, 1817, following the good-will visit to Boston of President James Monroe. The political bitterness declined because the Federalists had largely dissolved and were no longer attacking the president, then causing an Era of Good Feeling because there was only one political party.
Seminole War	The Seminole War s were three conflicts in Florida between various groups of Native Americans collectively known as Seminoles and the United States. The First Seminole War was from 1817 to 1818; the Second Seminole War from 1835 to 1842; and the Third Seminole War from 1855 to 1858. The Second Seminole War often referred to as the Seminole War lasted longer than any war involving the United States between the American Revolution and the Vietnam War.
McCulloch v. Maryland	McCulloch v. Maryland 17 U.S. 316 (1819), was a landmark decision by the Supreme Court of the United States. The state of Maryland had attempted to impede operation of a branch of the Second Bank of the United States by imposing a tax on all notes of banks not chartered in Maryland. Though the law, by its language, was generally applicable, the U.S. Bank was the only out-of-state bank then existing in Maryland, and the law is generally recognized as having specifically targeted the U.S. Bank.
Robert Fulton	Robert Fulton was a U.S. engineer and inventor, who was widely credited with developing the first steam-powered ship marked as a commercial success. In 1800 he was commissioned by Napoleon Bonaparte to design Nautilus, which was the first practical submarine in history.

33

Thomas Gibbons	Thomas Gibbons was the Philadelphia Police Department Commissioner appointed by Mayor Joseph S. Clark Jr . in 1952. He was described as "incorruptible" and a "lone wolf" for his intense efforts against the La Cosa Nostra, specifically Angelo Bruno, and the corrupt police officers who supported it.
Corrupt Bargains	Three deals cut in connection with the presidency of the United States--two in contested United States presidential elections and a presidential appointment of a vice president--have been described as Corrupt Bargains Votes in the Electoral College, 1824. The voting by state in the House of Representatives, 1825. Note that all of Clay"s states voted for Adams.
	In the U.S. presidential election of 1824, no candidate was able to secure the required number of the electoral votes, thereby putting the outcome in the hands of the House of Representatives, which (to the surprise of many) elected John Quincy Adams over rival Andrew Jackson.

Dorr Rebellion	The Dorr Rebellion (1841-1842) was a short-lived armed insurrection in Rhode Island, in the United States, led by Thomas Wilson Dorr, who was agitating for changes to the state"s electoral system. Under Rhode Island"s charter, originally received in 1663, only landowners could vote. At the time, when most of the citizens of the colonies were farmers, this was considered fairly democratic.
New York	New York is a state in the Mid-Atlantic and Northeastern regions of the United States and is the nation"s third most populous. The state is bordered by New Jersey and Pennsylvania to the south, and Connecticut, Massachusetts and Vermont to the east. The state has a maritime border with Rhode Island east of Long Island, as well as an international border with the Canadian provinces of Quebec and Ontario to the northwest.
Spoils system	In the politics of the United States, a spoils system refers to an informal practice by which a political party, after winning an election, gives government jobs to its voters as a reward for working toward victory, and as an incentive to keep working for the party. It is opposed to a system of awarding offices on the basis of some measure of merit independent of political activity (merit system).
Jacksonian democracy	Jacksonian democracy refers to the political philosophy of United States President Andrew Jackson and his supporters. Jackson"s policies followed the era of Jeffersonian democracy which dominated the previous political era. Prior to and during Jackson"s time as President, his supporters (considered a precursor to today"s modern Democratic Party) were resisted by the rival Adams and Anti-Jacksonian factions, which later gave rise to the Whigs.
Nullification crisis	The Nullification Crisis was a sectional crisis during the presidency of Andrew Jackson around the question of whether a state can refuse to recognize or to enforce a federal law passed by the United States Congress. It was precipitated by protective tariffs, specifically the Tariff of 1828. The issue incited a debate over states" rights that ultimately threatened violent hostilities between South Carolina and the federal government, and the dissolution of the Union.
Black Hawk War	The Black Hawk War was fought in 1832 in the Midwestern United States. The war was named for Black Hawk, a war chief of the Sauk, Fox, and Kickapoo Native Americans, whose British Band fought against the United States Army and militia from Illinois and the Michigan Territory (present-day Wisconsin) for possession of lands in the area. Governor of Indiana Territory William Henry Harrison negotiated a treaty in 1804 with a group of Sauk and Fox leaders that ceded lands east of Mississippi River "forever".
Indian Territory	The Indian Territory The Indian Territory or the Indian territories, was land set aside within the United States for the use of Native Americans. The general borders were set by the Indian Intercourse Act of 1834. The Indian Territory had its roots in the British Royal Proclamation of 1763, which limited white settlement to Crown lands east of the Appalachian Mountains.
Trail of Tears	The Trail of Tears refers to the forced relocation in 1838 of the Cherokee Native American tribe to the Western United States, which resulted in the deaths of an estimated 4,000 Cherokees.

Osceola	Osceola was a war chief of the Seminole Indians in Florida. Osceola led a small band of warriors in the Seminole resistance during the Second Seminole War when the United States tried to remove the Seminoles from their lands. He exercized a great deal of influence on Micanopy, the highest ranking chief of the Seminoles.
Nicholas Biddle	Nicholas Biddle was one of the first five captains of the Continental Navy. As the American Revolution threatened to break out, he returned to the colonies and offered his services to the state of Pennsylvania. In August 1775, the Pennsylvania Committee of Safety placed Nicholas Biddle in command of the armed galley Franklin.
Whig Party	The Whig Party was a political party of the United States during the era of Jacksonian democracy. Considered integral to the Second Party System and operating from 1832 to 1856, the party was formed to oppose the policies of President Andrew Jackson and the Democratic Party.
Specie circular	The Specie Circular was an executive order issued by U.S. President Andrew Jackson in 1836 and carried out by President Martin Van Buren. It required payment for public lands be in gold and silver specie. The Act was a reaction to growing concerns about excessive speculation of land after the Indian Removal, most done with "soft money."
Log Cabin Campaign	The Log cabin campaign is a name given to the 1840 Presidential campaign of William Henry Harrison. Having tried unsuccessfully to become the new Whig Party"s only candidate for president in 1836 (he ended up being one of three), William Henry Harrison continued campaigning for the nomination until the next election cycle. At the December 1839 Whig convention, Harrison became the party"s official nominee for president.

New York Herald	The New York Herald was a large distribution newspaper based in New York City that existed between May 6, 1835 and 1924. The first issue of the paper was published by James Gordon Bennett, Sr.
Printing press	The printing press is a mechanical printing device for making copies of identical text on multiple sheets of paper. It was invented in Germany by the goldsmith Johannes Gutenberg in 1440.
Interchangeable parts	Interchangeable parts are parts that are for practical purposes identical. They are made to specifications that ensure that they are so nearly identical that they will fit into any device of the same type. One such part can freely replace another, without any custom fitting (such as filing.)

Puerto Rico	Puerto Rico , officially the Commonwealth of Puerto Rico , is a self-governing territory of the United States located in the northeastern Caribbean, east of the Dominican Republic and west of the Virgin Islands. Puerto Rico is composed of an archipelago that includes the main island of Puerto Rico and a number of smaller islands and keys, the largest of which are Vieques, Culebra, and Mona. The main island of Puerto Rico is the smallest by land area and second smallest by population among the four Greater Antilles.
Slave Codes	Slave codes were laws passed in colonial North America to regulate any state of subjection to a force, and were abolished after the U.S. Civil War. Slave codes authorized, indemnified or even required the use of violence and were long criticized by abolitionists for their brutality.
John Wesley Blassingame	John Wesley Blassingame (March 23, 1940 - February 13, 2000) was a scholar, historian, educator, writer, and leading pioneer in the study of American slavery. He was the former chairman of the African-American Studies program at Yale University. He died at age 59.
Eugene Dominic Genovese	Eugene Dominic Genovese is an American historian of the American South and American slavery. He has been noted for bringing a Marxist perspective to the study of power, class and relations between planters and slaves in the South. His work Roll, Jordan, Roll: The World the Slaves Made won the Bancroft Prize.
Herbert Gutman	Herbert Gutman (1928 - July 21, 1985) was a professor of history at the Graduate Center of the City University of New York, where he wrote on slavery and labor history. Gutman was born in 1928 to Jewish immigrant parents in New York City. His parents" leftism was deeply influential.
Peculiar Institution	"(Our) Peculiar institution" was a euphemism for slavery and the economic ramifications of it in the American South. The meaning of "peculiar" in this expression is "one"s own", that is, referring to something distinctive to or characteristic of a particular place or people. The proper use of the expression is always as a possessive, e.g., "our Peculiar institution" or "the South"s Peculiar institution".
Slavery	Slavery is a form of forced labor in which people are considered to be the property of others. Slaves can be held against their will from the time of their capture, purchase or birth, and deprived of the right to leave, to refuse to work and has existed to varying extents, forms and periods in almost all cultures and continents.
Walter Walford Johnson	Walter Walford Johnson (1904-04-16, to 1987-03-23) was a United States businessman and Democratic politician who served as the 32nd Governor of the State of Colorado from 1950 to 1951. 1904-04-16. He married Neva Morrow in 1922.

Ralph Waldo Emerson	Ralph Waldo Emerson was an American essayist, poet, and leader of the Transcendentalist movement in the early nineteenth century. He gradually drifted from the doctrines of his peers, then formulated and first expressed the philosophy of Transcendentalism in his 1836 essay, Nature.
Transcendentalism	Transcendentalism began as a protest against the general state of culture and society at the time, and in particular, the state of intellectualism at Harvard and the doctrine of the Unitarian church which was taught at Harvard Divinity School. Among their core beliefs was an ideal spiritual state that "transcends" the physical and empirical and is only realized through the individual"s intuition, rather than through the doctrines of established religions.
Samuel Langhorne Clemens	Samuel Langhorne Clemens, better known by the pen name Mark Twain, was an American author and humorist. Twain is most noted for his novels Adventures of Huckleberry Finn, which has since been called the Great American Novel, and The Adventures of Tom Sawyer. He is extensively quoted.
Walden	Walden by Henry David Thoreau is one of the best-known non-fiction books written by an American. Published in 1854, it details Thoreau"s life for two years, two months, and two days in second growth forest around the shores of Walden Pond, on land owned by Ralph Waldo Emerson, not far from his friends and family in Concord, Massachusetts.
Brook Farm	Brook Farm was a utopian experiment in communal living in the United States in the 1840s. It was founded by former Unitarian minister George Ripley and his wife Sophia Ripley at the Ellis Farm in West Roxbury, Massachusetts in 1841 and was inspired in part by the ideals of Transcendentalism, a religious and cultural philosophy based in New England. Founded as a joint stock company, it promised its participants a portion of the profits from the farm in exchange for performing an equal share of the work.
Oneida Community	The Oneida Community was a utopian commune founded by John H. Noyes in 1848 near Oneida, New York. The community followed the beliefs of Noyes including which he called Perfectionism. There were initially some forty-five members to the community.
Shakers	The Shakers, a Protestant religious denomination officially called the United Society of Believers in Christ"s Second Appearing, originated in Manchester, England in 1772 under the leadership of Mother Ann Lee, who moved the nine-person group to New York in 1774.
Temperance movement	The temperance movement attempted to greatly reduce the amount of alcohol consumed or even prohibit its production and consumption entirely. In predominantly Muslim countries, temperance is part of Islam. In predominantly Christian countries, forms of Christianity influenced by Wesleyan views on sanctification have strongly supported it at times. More specifically, religious or moralistic beliefs have often been the catalyst for temperance, though secular advocates do exist.
Phrenology	Phrenology is a theory which claims to be able to determine character, personality traits, and criminality on the basis of the shape of the head . Developed by German physician Franz Joseph Gall around 1800, and very popular in the 19th century, it is now discredited as a pseudoscience.

North Star	The North Star was an abolitionist newspaper founded in 1847 by Frederick Douglass in Rochester, New York. Douglass, a former slave and a prominent antislavery speaker and writer, gained a circulation of over 4,000 readers in the United States, Europe, and the Caribbean. Taking as its motto "Right is of no Sex — Truth is of no Color — God is the Father of us all, and we are all brethren," the North Star served as a forum not only for abolitionist views, but also supported the feminist movement and the emancipation of other oppressed groups.
Puerto Rico	Puerto Rico , officially the Commonwealth of Puerto Rico , is a self-governing territory of the United States located in the northeastern Caribbean, east of the Dominican Republic and west of the Virgin Islands. Puerto Rico is composed of an archipelago that includes the main island of Puerto Rico and a number of smaller islands and keys, the largest of which are Vieques, Culebra, and Mona. The main island of Puerto Rico is the smallest by land area and second smallest by population among the four Greater Antilles.
Prigg v. Pennsylvania	Prigg v. Pennsylvania was a United States Supreme Court case in which the court held that Federal law is superior to State law, and overturned the conviction of Edward Prigg as a result.
Underground railroad	The Underground Railroad was a network of clandestine routes by which African slaves in the 19th century United States attempted to escape to free states, or as far north as Canada, with the aid of abolitionists. The Underground Railroad has captured public imagination as a symbol of freedom, and it figures prominently in Black American history.
James Gillespie Birney	James Gillespie Birney (February 4, 1792 - November 25, 1857) was an abolitionist, politician and jurist born in Danville, Kentucky. From 1816 to 1818, he served in the Kentucky House of Representatives. In 1836, he started his abolitionist weekly publication in Cincinnati, Ohio titled The Philanthropist.

Davy Crockett	David Stern Crockett (August 17, 1786 - March 6, 1836) was a celebrated 19th-century American folk hero, frontiersman, soldier and politician; referred to in popular culture as Davy Crockett and often by the epithet "King of the Wild Frontier." He represented Tennessee in the U.S. House of Representatives, served in the Texas Revolution, and died at the Battle of the Alamo. His nickname was the stuff of legend, but in life he shunned the title "Davy" and referred to himself exclusively as "David." Crockett was born on August 17, 1786 near the Nolichucky River in what is now Greene County, Tennessee. A re-creation of his birthplace cabin stands in Davy Crockett Birthplace State Park along the Nolichucky near Limestone, Tennessee.
Oregon	Oregon is a state in the Pacific Northwest region of the United States. The area was inhabited by many indigenous tribes before the arrival of traders, explorers and settlers. The Oregon Territory was created in 1848 after American settlement began in earnest in the 1840s.
Oregon Trail	The Oregon Trail was one of the key overland migration routes on which pioneers traveled across the North American continent in wagons in order to settle new parts of the United States of America during the 19th century. The Oregon Trail helped the United States implement its cultural goal of Manifest Destiny, that is to build a great nation spanning the North American continent.
Santa Fe Trail	The Santa Fe Trail was an historic 19th century transportation route across southwestern North America connecting Missouri with Santa Fe, New Mexico. First used in 1821 by William Becknell, it served as a vital commercial and military highway until the introduction of the railroad to Santa Fe in 1880.
Treaty of Guadalupe Hidalgo	The Treaty of Guadalupe Hidalgo was the peace treaty that ended the Mexican-American War (1846–1848). The treaty provided for the Mexican Cession, in which Mexico ceded 1.36 million km² (525,000 square miles) to the United States in exchange for USD$15 million. The United States also agreed to take over $3.25 million in debts Mexico owed to American citizens.
Missouri Compromise	The Missouri Compromise was an agreement passed in 1820 between the pro-slavery and anti-slavery factions in the United States Congress, involving primarily the regulation of slavery in the western territories. It prohibited slavery in the former Louisiana Territory north of the parallel 36°30" north except within the boundaries of the proposed state of Missouri. Prior to the agreement, the House of Representatives had refused to accept this compromise and a conference committee was appointed.
Popular sovereignty	Popular sovereignty is the doctrine that government is created by and subject to the will of the people, who are the source of all political power.
Stephen A. Douglas	Stephen A. Douglas nicknamed the "Little Giant" was an American politician from the western state of Illinois, and was the Democratic Party nominee for President in 1860. He was largely responsible for the Compromise of 1850 that apparently settled slavery issues. However in 1854 he reopened the slavery question by the highly controversial Kansas Nebraska Act that allowed the people of the new territories to decide for themselves whether or not to have slavery.

Ostend Manifesto	The Ostend Manifesto was a secret document written in 1854 by U.S. diplomats at Ostend, Belgium, describing a plan to acquire Cuba from Spain. The document declared that "Cuba is as necessary to the North American republic as any of its present members, and that it belongs naturally to that great family of states of which the Union is the Providential Nursery."
Bleeding Kansas	Bleeding Kansas Bloody Kansas or the Border War, was a series of violent events, involving anti-slavery Free-Staters and pro-slavery "Border Ruffian" elements, that took place in the Kansas Territory and the western frontier towns of the U.S. state of Missouri roughly between 1854 and 1858. At the heart of the conflict was the question of whether Kansas would enter the Union as a free state or slave state. As such, Bleeding Kansas was a proxy war between Northerners and Southerners over the issue of slavery in the United States.
Andrew Pickens Butler	Andrew Pickens Butler (November 18, 1796 - May 25, 1857) was an United States Senator and one of the authors of the Kansas-Nebraska Act. Butler was a son of William Butler, and was born in Edgefield County, South Carolina. His early education was at Moses Waddel"s Willington Academy.
Pottawatomie Massacre	The Pottawatomie Massacre occurred during the night of May 24 and the morning of May 25, 1856. In reaction to the sacking of Lawrence by pro-slavery forces, John Brown and a band of abolitionist settlers killed five pro-slavery settlers north of Pottawatomie Creek in Franklin County, Kansas. This was one of the many bloody episodes in Kansas preceding the American Civil War, which came to be known collectively as Bleeding Kansas.
Thomas R. Dew	Thomas R. Dew was an American educator and writer. He was well respected in the South; his widely distributed writings helped to confirm pro-slavery public opinion. He described the hardships faced by men in the marketplace and the almost brutal strength needed to survive in such a competetive atmosphere.
Dred Scott v. Sandford	Dred Scott v. Sandford 60 U.S. (19 How.) 393 (1857), was a decision by the United States Supreme Court that ruled that people of African descent imported into the United States and held as slaves, or their descendants--whether or not they were slaves--were not protected by the Constitution and could never be citizens of the United States. It also held that the United States Congress had no authority to prohibit slavery in federal territories.
Lincoln-Douglas debates	The Lincoln-Douglas debates of 1858 were a series of seven debates between Abraham Lincoln, the Republican candidate, and the incumbent Stephen A. Douglas, a Democrat, for an Illinois seat in the United States Senate. At the time, U.S. Senators were elected by state legislatures; thus Lincoln and Douglas were campaigning for their respective parties to win control of the Illinois legislature. The debates previewed the issues that Lincoln would face in the 1860 presidential election.

American Civil War	Although a territory of the British Empire, during the American Civil War the Bahamas were affected by the great conflict. Much as in the age of pirates the Bahamas were a haven for the swashbucklers, between 1861 to 1865 the Bahamas were a haven for blockade runners aligned with the Confederate States of America. Although Florida is still only 55 miles away, the state had few ports of any real consequence at the time.
Ohio idea	The Ohio idea was an idea by poor Midwesterners during the US presidential election of 1868 to redeem federal war bonds in United States dollars rather than gold. Agrarian Democrats hoped to keep more money in circulation to keep interest rates lower. In summary, wealthy eastern delegates demanded a plank promising that federal war bonds be redeemed in gold-even though many of the bonds had been purchased with badly depreciated paper greenbacks.
Union Party	The Union Party was a short-lived political party in the United States, formed in 1936 by a coalition of radio priest Father Charles Coughlin, old-age pension advocate Francis Townsend, and Gerald L. K. Smith, who had taken control of Huey Long"s Share Our Wealth movement after Long"s assassination in 1935. Each of those people hoped to channel their wide followings into support for the Union Party, which proposed a populist alternative to the New Deal reforms of Franklin D. Roosevelt during the Great Depression.
Confiscation Act	The Confiscation Act s were laws passed by the United States government during the Civil War with the intention of freeing the slaves still held by the Confederate forces in the South. The First Confiscation Act of 1861 authorized the confiscation of any Confederate property by Union forces ("property" included slaves.) This meant that all slaves that fought or worked for the Confederate military were freed whenever they were "confiscated" by Union troops.
Emancipation Proclamation	The Emancipation Proclamation consists of two executive orders issued by United States President Abraham Lincoln during the American Civil War. The first one, issued September 22, 1862, declared the freedom of all slaves in any state of the Confederate States of America that did not return to Union control by January 1, 1863. The second order, issued January 1, 1863, named ten specific states where it would apply.
United States Sanitary Commission	The United States Sanitary Commission was not an official agency of the United States government, created by legislation signed by President of the United States Abraham Lincoln on June 18, 1861, to coordinate the volunteer efforts of women who wanted to contribute to the war effort of the Union states during the American Civil War.
United States Military Academy	The United States Military Academy, also known as West Point, is a United States Army post and service academy. West Point was first a military post under the command of Benedict Arnold. Established in 1802, it is the oldest military academy in the United States.
Virginia	The Commonwealth of Virginia is an American state on the Atlantic Coast of the Southern United States. The state was named Virginia after Queen Elizabeth I of England, who was known as the "Virgin Queen" because she never married. The state is also known as the "Old Dominion" and sometimes "Mother of Presidents", because it is the birthplace of eight U.S. presidents.

Alabama claims	The Alabama Claims were a series of claims for damages by the United States government against the government of Great Britain for the covert assistance given to the Confederate cause during the American Civil War. After arbitration, in 1872 Britain paid the U.S. $15.5 million for damages done by warships built in Britain and sold to the Confederacy, thus ending the dispute and ensuring friendly relations. During the American Civil War, Confederate commerce raiders (the most famous being the CSS Alabama) were built in Britain and did significant damage to the American and merchant marine.
Albert Sidney Johnston	Albert Sidney Johnston (February 2, 1803 - April 6, 1862) was a career United States Army officer, a Texas Army general, and a Confederate States general. He saw extensive combat during his military career, fighting actions in the Texas War of Independence, the Mexican-American War, the Utah War, as well as the American Civil War. Considered by Confederate President Jefferson Davis to be the finest general officer in the Confederacy before the emergence of Robert E. Lee, he was killed early in the Civil War at the Battle of Shiloh and was the highest ranking officer, Union or Confederate, killed during the entire war.

Wade-Davis Bill	The Wade-Davis Bill of 1864 was a program proposed for the Reconstruction of the South written by two Radical Republicans, Senator Benjamin Wade of Ohio and Representative Henry Winter Davis of Maryland. In contrast to President Abraham Lincoln"s more lenient Ten percent plan, the bill made re-admittance to the Union almost impossible since it required a majority in each Southern state to swear the Ironclad oath to the effect they had never in the past supported the Confederacy. The bill passed both houses of Congress on July 2, 1864, but was vetoed by Lincoln and never took effect.
William A. Dunning	William A. Dunning was an American historian who founded the Dunning School of Reconstruction historiography at Columbia University, where he had graduated in 1881. The interpretation of post-Civil War Reconstruction in the United States that he and his students propounded was the dominant theory taught in American schools for the first half of the 20th century.
John Hope Franklin	John Hope Franklin (2 January 1915 - 25 March 2009) was a United States historian and past president of Phi Beta Kappa, the Organization of American Historians, the American Historical Association, and the Southern Historical Association. The John Matthews Manly Distinguished Service Professor Emeritus at The University of Chicago, Franklin is best known for his work From Slavery to Freedom, first published in 1947, and continually updated. More than three million copies have been sold.
Leon F. Litwack	Leon F. Litwack is an American historian and Professor of American History Emeritus at the University of California Berkeley, where he received the Golden Apple Award for Outstanding Teaching in 2007. He has received the Pulitzer Prize in History for his book Been In the Storm So Long: The Aftermath of Slavery.; he is the winner of the 1980 Francis Parkman Prize and the 1981 National Book Award . He is the recipient of a Guggenheim Fellowship and a National Endowment for the Humanities Film Grant.
Tenure of Office Act	The Tenure of Office Act, denied the President of the United States the power to remove from office anyone who had been appointed by the President by and with the advice and consent of the United States Senate unless the Senate also approved the removal.
Sharecropping	Sharecropping is a system of agricultural production where a landowner allows a farmer to use the land in return for a share of the crop produced on the land. Sharecropping has a long history, and there are a wide range of different situations and types of agreements that have encompassed the system. Some are governed by tradition, others by law.
New York Tribune	New York Tribune was established by Horace Greeley in 1841 and was long considered one of the leading newspapers in the United States.
Spoils system	In the politics of the United States, a spoils system refers to an informal practice by which a political party, after winning an election, gives government jobs to its voters as a reward for working toward victory, and as an incentive to keep working for the party. It is opposed to a system of awarding offices on the basis of some measure of merit independent of political activity (merit system).

Ohio idea	The Ohio idea was an idea by poor Midwesterners during the US presidential election of 1868 to redeem federal war bonds in United States dollars rather than gold. Agrarian Democrats hoped to keep more money in circulation to keep interest rates lower. In summary, wealthy eastern delegates demanded a plank promising that federal war bonds be redeemed in gold-even though many of the bonds had been purchased with badly depreciated paper greenbacks.
Resumption Act	The Resumption Act provided for the redemption of United States paper currency, known colloquially as greenbacks, in gold beginning in 1879. Drafted by Ohio Senator John Sherman, the Resumption Act was drafted in opposition to the Eastern financial community, who objected to how the act allowed the Treasury Secretary to manipulate the money supply.
Alabama claims	The Alabama Claims were a series of claims for damages by the United States government against the government of Great Britain for the covert assistance given to the Confederate cause during the American Civil War. After arbitration, in 1872 Britain paid the U.S. $15.5 million for damages done by warships built in Britain and sold to the Confederacy, thus ending the dispute and ensuring friendly relations. During the American Civil War, Confederate commerce raiders (the most famous being the CSS Alabama) were built in Britain and did significant damage to the American and merchant marine.
Knights of the White Camellia	The Knights of the White Camellia was a secret group opposing the carpetbaggers in the U.S. Southern states during the Reconstruction era and beyond. Like most of such groups, it was founded by a Confederate veteran, as veterans represented most of southern white men. Col.
Red Shirts	The Red Shirts were the supporters of Wade Hampton in the South Carolina gubernatorial elections of 1876 and 1878. They came to symbolize a revived Southern Nationalism and the redemption of the state from Radical Republican rule during Reconstruction.
Treaty of Washington	The Treaty of Washington was a treaty negotiated between the United Kingdom and the United States in 1871. The treaty dealt with grievances stemming from the American Civil War and cross-border issues with the newly-formed Dominion of Canada.
Rutherford B. Hayes	Rutherford B. Hayes, 19th President, became president after the tumultuous, scandal-ridden years of the Grant administration. In domestic affairs, aside from reconciliation with the South, his administration was noteworthy for two achievements, both giving evidence of a strong president resolute in his relations with Congress: resumption of specie (mainly gold) backing of the paper currency and bonds that financed the war, and the beginning of civil service reform.
Samuel J. Tilden	Samuel J. Tilden was a Democratic candidate for the U.S. presidency in the disputed election of 1876, the most controversial American election of the 19th century. A political reformer, he was a Bourbon Democrat who worked closely with the New York City business community, led the fight against the corruption of Tammany Hall, and fought to keep taxes low.

New South	New South is a term that has been used intermittently since the American Civil War to describe the American South, in whole or in part. The term "New South" is often used in contrast to the Old South of the antebellum period.
Redeemers	The Redeemers were a political coalition in the Southern United States during the Reconstruction era, who sought to overthrow the Radical Republican coalition of Freedmen, carpetbaggers and Scalawags. They were the southern wing of the Bourbon Democrats, the conservative, pro-business wing of the Democratic Party.
Jim Crow laws	Discriminatory Anti-miscegenation Â· Anti-immigration Alien and Sedition Acts Â· Jim Crow laws BR>Test Act Â· Apartheid laws Ketuanan Melayu Â· Nuremberg Laws Diyya Â· Anti-homelessness legislation LGBT rights by country or territory Anti-discriminatory Anti-discrimination acts Â· Anti-discrimination law Â· 14th Amendment Â· 19th Amendment Â· Crime of apartheid CERD Â· CEDAW Â· CDE Â· ILO C111 Â· ILO C100

Other forms

Adultcentrism Â· Androcentrism Â· Anthropocentrism Â·
Colorism Â· Cronyism Â· Ethnocentrism Â·
Economic Â· Genism Â· Gynocentrism
Linguicism Â· Nepotism Â· Triumphalism

Related topics

A bus station in Durham, North Carolina, in May 1940.

Bigotry Â· Diversity Â·
Eugenics Â· Eurocentrism
Multiculturalism Â· Oppression
Political correctness Â· Prejudice
Stereotype Â· Tolerance

	The Jim Crow laws were state and local laws in the United States enacted between 1876 and 1965. They mandated de jure segregation in all public facilities, with a supposedly "separate but equal" status for black Americans. In reality, this led to treatment and accommodations that were usually inferior to those provided for white Americans, systematizing a number of economic, educational and social disadvantages.
Plessy v. Ferguson	Plessy v. Ferguson, 163 U.S. 537 - 1896, was a landmark United States Supreme Court decision in the jurisprudence of the United States, upholding segregation and the constitutionality of the "separate but equal" doctrine.

Tuskegee Institute	Tuskegee Institute is an American institution of higher learning located in Tuskegee, Alabama. The school was the dream of Lewis Adams, a former slave and George W. Campbell, a former slave owner. In 1941, in an effort to train black aviators, a training squadron of the U.S. Army Air Corps was established at Tuskegee Institute.
Poll tax	A poll tax is a tax of a uniform, fixed amount per individual as opposed to a percentage of income. Such taxes were important sources of revenue for many countries into the 19th century, but this is no longer the case.

Capital

Flag

Djibouti

Language(s)	French, Arabic
Religion	Islam, Christianity
Government	Overseas territory of France
High Commissioner	
- 1967-1969	Louis Saget
- 1969-1971	Dominique Ponchardier
- 1971-1974	Georges Thiercy
- 1974-1976	Christian Dablanc
- 1976-1977	Camille d"Ornano
Historical era	Cold War
- Established	July 5, 1967
- Independence	June 27, 1977
Area	
- 1974	23,200 km^2
Population	
- 1974 est.	200,000
Density	8.6 /km^2 (22.3 /sq mi)
Currency	Djiboutian franc

The French Territory of Afars and Issas is the name given to the territory of present-day Republic of Djibouti during the French colonial rule between 1967 and independence in 1977. The name took into account the two peoples majority of the territory: the Afars and the Issas.

The original territorial land on the north side of Gulf of Tadjoura was called Obock Territory (Territoire d"Obock) from 1862 to 1894.

LaVergne, TN USA
28 April 2010
180846LV00002B/194/P

9 781616 540616